MENTAL TOUGHNESS AFFIRMATIONS FOR TEEN GIRLS

---

101 AFFIRMATIONS TO FOSTER GRIT, RESILIENCE, POSITIVE SELF-TALK & A GROWTH MINDSET FOR OPTIMAL PERFORMANCE AND WELL-BEING

Y.D. GARDENS

THE EMERALD
SOCIETY

A SPECIAL GIFT TO MY READERS

Visit emeraldsocpublishing.com to download your FREE copy!

LEAVE A REVIEW

Don't forget to share the love
&
leave your Amazon review for:

INTRODUCTION

H ey girl!

WELCOME to a world where your voice is your superpower, and your thoughts are the magic that shapes your reality. You're holding a book that's more than just pages and words—it's a toolkit for building an unstoppable you. We're talking about mental toughness, unshakeable grit, and resilience that bounces back stronger every time. And the coolest part? You're going to harness these powers with something as simple, yet as mighty, as affirmations.

Let's face it, being a teen today is like being a superhero in a really complex world. You're juggling school, friendships, maybe love (or the annoying lack of it), family dynamics, and all those wild dreams and fears about the future. Sometimes, it feels like you're climbing a mountain with no peak in sight. But what if you had secret weapons that could transform those struggles into your greatest strengths? That's where a growth mindset and the art of affirmations come in.

First off, a growth mindset is this rad concept that your abilities and intelligence aren't set in stone. They're more like clay, ready to be molded by your hands. It means looking at challenges and saying, "Bring it on!" instead of "Why me?". It's about understanding that failing doesn't make you a failure—it makes you a fierce learner.

Now, let's talk about affirmations. Think of them as your personal hype playlist, but for your brain. Affirmations are powerful, positive statements that you tell yourself to challenge and overcome self-sabotaging and negative thoughts. When you repeat them, believe in them, and live by them, something magical happens. Your brain starts rewiring itself. It's like programming a computer—your affirmations are the code that tells your mind, "Hey, we're strong, capable, and ready to conquer the world!"

Imagine starting each day by telling yourself, "I am brave enough to tackle any challenge," or "I grow stronger with every obstacle I face." These aren't just feel-good words; they're your armor and shield as you go out to face the world. Every time you affirm your strength, your worth, and your power, you're not just saying it, you're building it within you.

In this book, you'll explore 101 statements to strengthen your mind. This will have an impact on the way your think (obviously!) but also extend to your relationships, self-perception, as well as your emotional and physical health.

Developing a growth mindset through affirmations will empower you to rise above challenges and step into the strongest version of yourself. As you move through these pages, you'll also have the opportunity to use the space below each affirmation to practice intuitive journaling, a potent method of releasing emotions and manifesting your desires. You will be guided to reflect on each statement as they resonate with your soul, speak to your struggles, and celebrate your uniqueness.

Together, we'll embark on this journey of transforming your mindset, one affirmation at a time.

So, are you ready to unlock the power within you? Are you excited to reprogram your mind for greatness? Let's turn these pages and start building a resilient, empowered, and unstoppable you. The world better watch out, because here you come, armed with your affirmations and a mindset that can move mountains!

WELCOME TO YOUR POWER. Let's start this beautiful adventure.

TIPS & REMINDERS...

Navigating the intricate maze of adolescence is no easy feat, and affirmations are one of the many tools you can use to find your way. As you journey through this book and start embracing the power of mental toughness affirmations, please keep in mind that real change takes time, patience, and consistency. As such, I've compiled a short list of additional pointers to keep in mind, ensuring you make the most of these affirmations.

1. **Consistency is Key:** Saying an affirmation once is good; making it a daily ritual is transformative. Regular repetition will enhance their impact on your mindset.
2. **Be Patient and Kind to Yourself:** Changing deeply ingrained beliefs and thought patterns won't happen overnight. Be patient, and remember to treat yourself with the same kindness you'd offer a dear friend.

3. **Feel Your Emotions:** As you recite an affirmation, try to genuinely feel its essence. Embody the emotion and visualize its truth manifesting in your life. Let your feelings - good or bad - flow through you, and greet them with loving compassion.

4. **Practice Mindfulness:** Combining affirmations with mindfulness practices like meditation or deep breathing can amplify their effects. This will help ground you and create a sense of calm.

5. **Journal Your Journey:** Journaling is proven to be a great way to build self-awareness and promote personal growth. You can use these pages to document your feelings, experiences, and progress.

6. **Celebrate Small Wins:** When you notice a change in your mood, perspective, or confidence level, celebrate it! Every step forward, no matter how tiny, is progress.

7. **Seek Professional Help if Needed**: If you're struggling intensely with self-esteem or body image issues, or if feelings of sadness and hopelessness persist, it's essential to seek professional guidance. Affirmations are a tool, but therapy or counseling might provide deeper insights and a variety of healthy coping strategies.

Your journey of personal growth and empowerment is unique, beautiful, and ever-evolving.

As you move forward, remember that the path isn't always linear.

There will be highs and lows, moments of doubt, and moments of unwavering confidence.

Embrace every phase, knowing that each experience contributes to the incredible tapestry of your life.

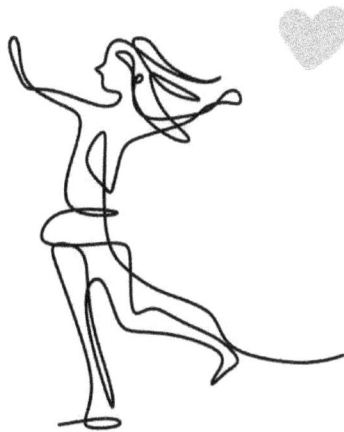

101 MENTAL TOUGHNESS
AFFIRMATIONS

> She believed she could, so she did.

R.S. GREY

1

I am resilient, and I bounce back from challenges stronger than
ever.

—❖—

2

My mind is a powerful force, and I use it to overcome any obstacles in my path.

———❖———

3

I embrace the process of improvement and trust that each step forward is a victory.

———❖———

4

I am in control of my thoughts, and I choose positivity and strength.

———❖———

5

Every setback is a setup for a comeback; I use challenges as
stepping stones to success

❖

6

I am a fierce competitor, and I thrive under pressure.

———❖———

7

My determination is unwavering; I pursue my goals with relentless dedication.

—❖—

8

I am mentally tough, capable of pushing through discomfort to achieve greatness.

—❖—

9

Challenges are opportunities for growth, and I welcome them with open arms.

❖

10

I trust in my abilities and believe in my capacity to achieve anything I set my mind to.

❖

11

I am disciplined and committed to putting in the work necessary to reach my full potential.

❖

12

I am a leader on and off the field, inspiring others with my resilience and dedication.

— ❖ —

13

My mindset is my greatest asset; I cultivate a positive attitude in all aspects of my life.

—❖—

14

I face adversity with courage, knowing it only makes me stronger in the end.

—❖—

15

I am the architect of my destiny, shaping my future with determination and focus.

———❖———

16

I am unshakeable; no external factors can disrupt my inner peace and confidence.

❖

17

I celebrate my successes, big and small, recognizing the progress I make every day.

—❖—

18

My passions fuel my perseverance; I am dedicated to constant improvement.

---- ❖ ----

19

I am not defined by setbacks; I am defined by my ability to rise above them.

❖

20

I am a master of my thoughts, choosing positivity and strength in every situation.

❖

21

I trust the process and understand that success is a journey, not a destination.

———❖———

22

I am a champion, and my mindset reflects the qualities of a true winner.

———❖———

23

I approach challenges with a calm and focused mind, finding solutions with ease.

—❖—

24

My perseverance sets me apart, allowing me to excel under any circumstances.

—❖—

25

I am a warrior, facing adversity with courage and determination.

❖

26

I am a source of inspiration to others, demonstrating the power of resilience.

❖

27

I am unstoppable; no challenge is too great for my indomitable spirit.

————— ❖ —————

28

I cultivate a mindset of gratitude, appreciating the journey and the lessons it brings.

❖

29

I am filled with positivity, radiating strength and encouragement
to those around me.

❖

30

I am disciplined in my habits, creating a foundation for success in everything I set my mind to.

—❖—

31

I approach each task with focus and determination, making the most of every opportunity.

———❖———

32

I am a constant learner, seeking wisdom and knowledge to enhance my skills.

—❖—

33

I trust in my efforts and preparation, confident in my ability to perform at my best.

❖

34

I am a problem solver, finding solutions even in the face of adversity.

———❖———

35

I am a champion in the making, with the resilience to overcome any challenge.

——✤——

36

I visualize success and manifest my goals through the power of positive thinking.

———❖———

37

I am in control of my reactions; I choose to respond with grace and determination.

———❖———

38

My self-belief is unwavering, and I approach each challenge with confidence.

—❖—

39

I am strong, inspiring others to reach new heights.

———❖———

40

I am a student of life, always seeking to improve.

— ❖ —

41

I am mentally unbreakable, rising above challenges with grace and resilience.

———❖———

42

I trust in my ability to adapt and adjust, staying calm under pressure.

—❖—

43

I am a source of motivation, pushing myself and others to achieve greatness.

— ❖ —

44

I move forward with a relentless spirit, never giving up on my dreams.

—❖—

45

I am a role model for perseverance, showing others the power of a determined mindset.

——❖——

46

I embrace discomfort as a sign of growth, pushing my limits to become the best person I can be.

❖

47

I am a force to be reckoned with, approaching each challenge with confidence and poise.

———❖———

48

I am a master of my emotions, channeling them into focused and
purposeful energy.

———❖———

49

I am resilient, turning setbacks into comebacks with determination and grit.

———❖———

50

I am a leader who sets an example of mental toughness for others.

—❖—

51

I thrive under pressure, using it as fuel to elevate my performance to new heights.

———❖———

52

I am disciplined, committed to the daily grind that leads to success.

—❖—

53

I trust in my instincts, confident that they guide me toward the right decisions.

❖

54

I am a problem-solving girl, finding solutions in the midst of challenges.

❖

55

I am filled with positivity, spreading encouragement and strength around me.

❖

56

I am a young woman with a warrior spirit, facing challenges head-on.

—❖—

57

I am a constant learner, always seeking ways to improve and grow.

❖

58

I am a strategic thinker, approaching life with intelligence and mindfulness.

———❖———

59

I am a source of inspiration, motivating myself and others to reach their full potential.

❖

60

I am a champion in the making, with the mental toughness to overcome any hurdle.

— ❖ —

61

I approach challenges as opportunities to fuel my determination.

❖

62

I am committed to constant improvement.

———❖———

63

I use my individuality and uniqueness to achieve my goals.

———❖———

64

I am kind to myself as I work through challenges.

———❖———

65

My never-give-up attitude allows me to push through difficult times.

———— ❖ ————

66

Opportunities for growth and success are everywhere.

———❖———

67

I am a visionary, seeing success in my mind's eye and working hard
to achieve it.

---❖---

68

I am a focused learner, giving my best effort in everything I set my mind to.

———❖———

69

I am the master of my thoughts and emotions.

—❖—

70

I let go of all limiting beliefs.

—❖—

71

I am a positive force in the face of adversity.

—❖—

72

I turn challenges into opportunities for growth.

—❖—

73

I cultivate thoughts that empower and uplift me.

——❖——

74

I am strong and courageous beyond measure.

———❖———

75

I am compassionate toward myself as I learn and grow.

———❖———

76

I am a constant seeker of improvement, always looking for ways to refine and enhance my skills.

❖

77

I have a winning mentality, approaching every aspect of life with confidence and trust in myself.

❖

78

I feel empowered to make positive choices.

—❖—

79

I am a source of inspiration, motivating myself and those around me to reach new heights.

❖

80

I am a champion, and my mental toughness sets me apart from the rest.

———— ❖ ————

81

I am a positive leader, setting an example of kindness, resilience and determination for others.

—❖—

82

I embrace change and am constantly growing and evolving.

———❖———

83

I am a pursuer of personal excellence, committed to achieving my full potential.

———❖———

84

I have a knack for problem-solving, easily finding solutions in the face of challenges.

❖

85

I am proud of the person I am and the woman I am becoming.

— ❖ —

86

I radiate strength and encourage those around me.

—❖—

87

I take pride in my work ethic and always strive to do my best.

—❖—

88

I am a confident, kind and compassionate leader.

— ❖ —

89

I am a hard worker and am worthy of success and achievement.

❖

90

I can overcome any obstacle.

———❖———

91

I feed my mind with positive and encouraging words.

❖

92

I trust that I am on the right track, even when the path is unclear.

❖

93

I am in flow and open to whatever comes my way.

❖

94

My dreams become my goals, and these goals become my achievements.

—❖—

95

Every day, I am becoming a stronger and wiser version of myself.

———❖———

96

My mistakes are my greatest teachers.

❖

97

I know I am enough, just as I am, and am worthy of every success.

❖

98

My mindset is a powerful tool, and I choose positivity in every situation.

—❖—

99

I trust in my ability to overcome obstacles and emerge stronger.

— ❖ —

100

I am in control of my thoughts, focusing on what I can achieve
rather than what I can't.

❖

101

I am a persistent and tenacious individual, never giving up on my dreams.

———❖———

BONUS #1

I believe in my own capabilities and am confident in my capacity to handle any situation.

❖

BONUS #2

I approach challenges with a calm and focused mind, finding solutions with ease.

❖

BONUS #3

I celebrate my achievements, acknowledging the progress I make on my journey to greatness.

❖

RISE & SHINE

---

66 Your attitude, not your aptitude, will determine your altitude.

ZIG ZIGLAR

POSTSCRIPT

I'd love to hear your thoughts...

Hey, lovely!

As an independent author with a small marketing budget, **reviews** are my livelihood on this platform.

If you enjoyed this book, I would truly appreciate it if you left your honest feedback.

You can do this by clicking the link to this *Mental Toughness for Teen Girls* book on www.amazon.com.

Additionally, you can jump in and join our well-being community via https://www.facebook.com/groups/theemeraldsociety, or contact me directly at:
  ydgardens@emeraldsocpublishing.com.

I personally read every single review, and it warms my heart to hear from my readers.

With Kindness,
  Yas

THE EMERALD
S O C I E T Y

JOIN OUR TRIBE

Mental Toughness for Teen Girls:

101 Affirmations to Foster Grit, Resilience, Positive Self-Talk & a Growth Mindset for Optimal Performance and Well-Being

CHECK OUT OTHER BOOKS BY Y.D. GARDENS!

Growing Into You: A Guide to Living Authentically - Find Purpose and Belonging by Stepping Away from Your Shadow and Back into Yourself

Growing Stronger: Cultivate Inner Peace & Stand Out by Becoming the Best Version of Yourself

Awakening to Authenticity Collection: Find Purpose, Cultivate Inner Peace and Stand Out by Becoming the Best Version of Yourself

The Well-Being Handbook: A Complete Guide to Optimal Well-ness, Positive Habits & Holistic Self-Care

Manifesting The One: 101 Affirmations to Attract Your Soulmate and Manifest True & Abundant Love

Stepping Into The Shadows: 33 Things to Know Before Starting Your Shadow Healing Journey

Embracing Your Darkness: An Intuitive Woman's Guide to Empowerment, Holistic Healing & Spiritual Growth Through Shadow Work

Shadow Healing Journal & Workbook: 201 Powerful Affirmations to Support Your Mind, Body & Soul Throughout Your Shadow Work Journey

Self-Love Affirmations for Teen Girls: 101 Empowering Affirmations to Boost Self-Esteem, Improve Body Image, and Nurture Emotional Well-Being

NOW AVAILABLE!

And here's a sneak peek, just for you...

INTRODUCTION

E very single morning, as the sun awakens the world with its
golden touch, a mirror somewhere reflects the image of a
young girl trying to find her place in the vast universe.
Perhaps she notices a new pimple or some other natural imperfec-
tion, compares her body to a photoshopped model, or wishes she
were 'smarter,' 'prettier,' or simply 'better.'

Do you recognize this girl? Does her story sound familiar? If
so, then this book holds the magic to transform your reflections.

Here's an alarming truth: 7 out of 10 girls believe that they are
not good enough in some way. Whether it's their looks, grades, or
relationships, teenage years are tumultuous in many ways and can
be some of the most challenging times for self-worth.

The journey from adolescence to adulthood is a whirlwind of
emotions, changes, and challenges. Often, the loudest voice we
hear isn't that of friends, family, or the media but our own self-crit-
ical voice.

But what if that voice could be our greatest ally?

If you've picked up this book, chances are you, too, have felt the sting of self-doubt or have wished to see the person in the mirror a bit more kindly.

So, what do we mean when we talk about self-love and self-esteem? At its core, **self-love** is the appreciation, respect, and acceptance you have for yourself. It's about understanding that you are worthy, just as you are, and deserving of love, respect, and all the good things that life has to offer.

On the other hand, **self-esteem** is the confidence in your own worth and abilities. It's the silent whisper that tells you that you can, even when the world suggests you can't; a barometer of how much you value, approve of, and believe in yourself. Together, self-love and self-esteem form the foundation upon which we build our relationships, face challenges, and evolve into the incredible women we're destined to become.

Yet, in the cacophony of your teen years, amid the whirlwind of societal expectations, peer pressures, and personal aspirations, that whisper can become muted.

That's where **self-affirmations** come into play.

Like tiny seeds, when nurtured, these affirmations can grow into mighty trees of confidence and self-belief. Repeatedly telling yourself that you are strong, capable, and deserving not only drowns out the negative chatter but reprograms your brain, creating positive neural pathways.

These powerful, positive statements are so much more than just feel-good phrases; they are backed by science. And, as you grow into a confident, well-rounded young adult, these affirmations will become your armor against the world's challenges.

Trust me – I've been there.

As such, I offer you this book as a guide on your transformative journey. Through the following pages, you will find 101 powerful affirmations that aim to bolster your self-esteem, improve your body image, and nurture your emotional well-being. Each affirmation is a stepping stone to **uncover the real you**, leading toward a future where you see yourself as the unique, incredible individual you truly are.

Listen to these affirmations and read them time and again – the more repetition, the better. To take your self-love journey one step further, use this tool as a journal by recording your thoughts and feelings linked to each affirmation in the space provided on each page.

So, lovely, this is it: This book is your guide to the transformative world of self-affirmations, paving the path toward uncovering the best version of yourself.

These 101 affirmations were carefully curated to resonate with your unique challenges, desires, and aspirations - all that comes with being a teen girl!

Remember that you nurture your mind and soul by affirming your worth, thus creating a path to grow into a confident, happy, and well-rounded adult. Embrace this journey, for it is a beautiful one. And remember, the most important relationship you'll ever have is with yourself. Let's make it a loving one.

So, are you ready to embark on this journey of self-discovery, acceptance, and boundless love? Because the world needs you — in all your radiant, empowered glory.

To receive more **FREE books** by Y.D. Gardens, visit
emeraldsocpublishing.com

www.ingramcontent.com/pod-product-compliance
Lightning Source LLC
LaVergne TN
LVHW041258080426
835510LV00009B/789